OXFORD

WILD READS

D0631198

Horses

K. M. Peyton

OXFORD
UNIVERSITY PRESS

This book belongs to:

OXFORD
UNIVERSITY PRESS

Great Clarendon Street, Oxford OX2 6DP
Oxford University Press is a department of the University of Oxford.
It furthers the University's objective of excellence in research, scholarship,
and education by publishing worldwide in

Oxford   New York

Auckland   Cape Town   Dar es Salaam   Hong Kong   Karachi
Kuala Lumpur   Madrid   Melbourne   Mexico City   Nairobi
New Delhi   Shanghai   Taipei   Toronto

With offices in

Argentina   Austria   Brazil   Chile   Czech Republic   France   Greece
Guatemala   Hungary   Italy   Japan   Poland   Portugal   Singapore
South Korea   Switzerland   Thailand   Turkey   Ukraine   Vietnam

Oxford is a registered trade mark of Oxford University Press
in the UK and in certain other countries

Text © K. M. Peyton
Illustrations © Michael Langham Rowe
The moral rights of the author have been asserted

Database right Oxford University Press (maker)

This edition 2009

British Library Cataloguing in Publication Data

Data available

ISBN: 978-0-19-911972-1

1 3 5 7 9 10 8 6 4 2

Printed in China
Paper used in the production of this book is a natural,
recyclable product made from wood grown in sustainable forests.
The manufacturing process conforms to the environmental
regulations of the country of origin.

Contents

▶ Horses in the wild   4

▶ The horse is tamed   8

▶ The horse's lessons   10

▶ The horse in history   13

▶ Disaster!   18

▶ Different breeds   20

▶ Grooming your horse   25

▶ The horse in sport   26

▶ Just riding   27

▶ Glossary   30

▶ Horses in the wild

A herd of wild horses moves across the plain. There are about twenty of them, led by their stallion. Something has frightened them. They are restless. They can sense danger.

Their ears are sharp. They can hear distant voices, distant hooves. They stop grazing and start to move, following their stallion. First they walk, then the stallion breaks into a trot. The herd closes together in a tight bunch. The fear spreads and the trot becomes a canter. The canter becomes a gallop.

The wild horses know that men want to catch them and tame them to ride. But they do not want to be caught!

They are fast. They gallop altogether, they never split up. The earth shivers with the sound of drumming hooves. The dust rises in a great cloud. The herd leaps over the streams and rocks in its path.

But the men are driving them into a deep valley. At the end they have built a high, strong fence, too big for the horses to jump. They are captured!

▶ The horse is tamed

One man catches a horse with a rope. The horse kicks and rears and bucks, struggling to get free. But the man does not let him go. The horse gets tired and he knows he is beaten.

Mustang

Mustang

Now the man can make him do what he wants. He can get on his back and ride him. The man will keep him in a pen and reward him with feed. The man has tamed the horse.

There are not many herds of horses living in the wild today. They are kept by people now. Horses are very strong animals, stronger than any man, but not fierce. They like to please, and enjoy being with people.

The horse's lessons

At three years old a horse is fully grown and can begin work. He is "broken in" – this means he learns to have a saddle on his back and a bridle on his head. The horse usually kicks and bucks until he becomes used to the saddle. He is sometimes very ticklish!

saddle

The saddle is put on his back. The strap which holds the saddle in place is pulled tight round his tummy. It has to be tight or the saddle will move. This strap is called the girth.

girth

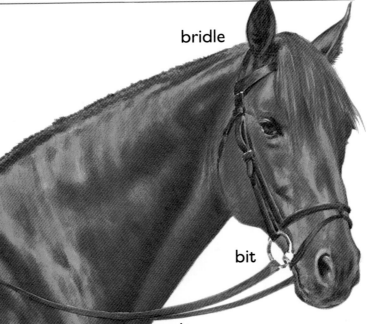

bridle

bit

reins

The bridle holds a steel bar
called a bit which lies in the horse's
mouth over its tongue. The bit
has reins which run to the rider's
hands. The rider steers the horse
with the reins and pulls on them
both to ask the horse to stop.

11

When the horse is used to the saddle
and bridle, the rider gets on his back
for the first time. But he has to do it
slowly. At first he just leans over the
saddle. When the horse is used to his
weight he starts to ride properly.

The first part of the horse's training
is over.

► The horse in history

A hundred and fifty years ago there were no cars, no trains, no aeroplanes, no coaches. There were only horses. You rode a horse, or you travelled in a cart or coach that the horse pulled. Or, if you were poor, you walked.

Horses were used for everything. They worked on the farms. They pulled the plough to turn the earth. They pulled the reaper that cut the corn and hay. They pulled great wagons that carried the corn and hay to the barns. They pulled the carts carrying food to market to sell.

a Suffolk pulls
a plough

horses pulling a stagecoach

In the towns horses pulled the coaches and carts to take people to work. They worked in pairs or fours for the big loads. They travelled long distances in "stages". The people got on the coach and every ten miles the four horses were changed for four fresh horses. In this way, they could travel at ten miles an hour.

In the towns there were traffic jams just like there are today. But the traffic was all horses.

horse-drawn traffic in the town

Did you know...
There were stables everywhere, like petrol stations today.

Men would ride from town to town to visit or work. A fit horse could carry a man 50 miles in a day.

Women rode too. They rode side-saddle, with both legs on the same side of the horse. It was more comfortable (not for the horse though!)

Children loved to ride and often rode ponies to school.

the Palomino

Disaster!

But then man invented the engine.

He invented the train for long distances. Then he invented the car, then the tractor.

After thousands of years of work, horses were not needed any more. The tractor took the place of the horse on the farm. The train took the place of the horse-drawn carriage. The car took the place of the horse in the town.

But people had learned to love the horse. They did not want to give him up. They decided to keep the horse, not for work, but for sport and enjoyment.

▶ Different breeds

There are many breeds of horse, like breeds of dogs.

The Arab

The Arab is the oldest breed. It has a beautiful head, large eyes, fine legs and a long silky mane and tail. It is sparky by nature, and can be a lively ride.

the Arab

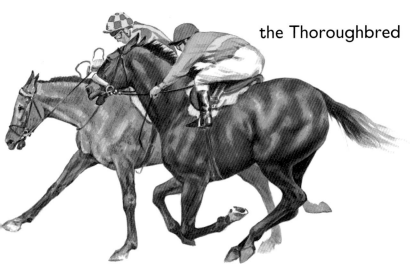

The Thoroughbred

The Thoroughbred is a bigger, faster, finer Arab. It was bred in England for racing. It is now a separate breed. Horses love racing. They gallop in a herd as if they are wild again.

The Cob

The Cob is a chunky small horse with thick legs. It is very sensible and can be used for anything. Children can ride it or it can pull a cart.

the Cob

21

the Welsh pony

The Welsh pony

The Welsh pony is small and very pretty. It is very good for children to ride.

In Britain there are several breeds of small ponies. They still live wild in herds. They live on Exmoor, Dartmoo in the New Forest and on the Fells. The smallest pony is the Shetland.

Did you know...
A pony is a small horse. Some people think a small pony will grow into a horse. But it doesn't. It is a small breed.

The Shire

The biggest breeds are the carthorses.
The Shire is the biggest of all.
A Shetland can walk under a Shire's
tummy!

the Shire

the Shetland

Horses' colours

Horses are mostly brown or black or grey. Bay is the commonest colour.

A bright brown with a black mane and tail is called a bay.

A bright brown with a red mane and tail is called a chestnut.

A black and white horse is called a piebald.

A brown and white horse is called a skewbald.

A grey horse grows white when it is old. Horses live about 25 years.

▶ Grooming your horse

A horse is groomed to keep its coat clean and shining.

Dandy brush
hard brush for mud, mane and tail

Body brush
finer brush to groom coat with

Mane comb
comb to tidy the mane

Hoof pick
to pick dirt and stones wedged in feet

Curry comb
to clean the body brush on

Plaited tail for best occasions

The horse in sport

Racing and jumping are very popular. The horse is a natural jumper. In the wild it jumped whatever was in its path.

A good showjumper can jump almost two metres high!

Did you know...
If a horse trusts you and you ask him to jump into a lake, he will do it, even if he can't see how deep it is.

▶ Just Riding

Many people keep a horse just to ride. You can ride along the lanes, through the woods, gallop over the downs. You can ride over the mountains or across the plains.

The horse trusts you. You groom
him and feed him hay and corn.
You give him a field to graze in and
a warm stable when it is cold with a
thick bed of straw or sawdust.

The horse has come a long way from
his life in the wild when he thought
of man as his enemy.

 Glossary

 breed A breed means a kind of horse. **20, 21, 22, 23**

 buck When a horse bucks, it puts its head down and kicks up its back legs. **8, 10**

 canter The canter is faster than a trot, and slower than a gallop. **5**

 gallop The gallop is the fastest pace that a horse can go. **5, 6, 21, 27**

 graze To graze means to eat growing grass. **5, 28**

 groom To groom means to brush a horse's coat to make it clean. **25, 28**

hoof A hoof is the hard shell round a horse's foot.

5, 6, 11, 25

 rear When a horse rears, it stands right up on its hind legs.

8

 stallion A stallion is a male horse.

4, 5

 trot A trot is the next pace up from walk, like a human jogging.

5

OXFORD

WILD READS

WILD READS will help your child develop a love of reading and
a lasting curiosity about our world. See the websites and places
to visit below to learn more about horses.

Horses

WEBSITES
http://games.pcuk.org/

BOOKS
K. M. Peyton, who wrote this book, has also written a fiction series;
a great family saga with the main character's love of horses at the heart of the first book.
Flambards, The Edge of the Cloud, Flambards in Summer and *Flambards Divided.*

PLACES TO VISIT
HorseWorld Visitors Centre
http://www.horseworld.org.uk/visitorcentre/

There are still some wild horses living in England.
They live on Exmoor, Dartmoor, in the New Forest and on the Fells.